Is This Normal?

MORE Girls' questions, answered by the editors of

The Care & Keeping of YOU

illustrated by Josée Masse

⭐ American Girl®

Published by American Girl Publishing

18 19 20 21 22 23 24 QP 10 9 8 7 6 5 4 3 2 1

Editorial Development: Darcie Johnston
Art Direction and Design: Jessica Rogers
Production: Jeannette Bailey, Tami Kepler, Judith Lary, Kristi Lively, Paula Moon
Illustrations: Josée Masse

Special thanks to Jane Annunziata, Psy.D., and Cara Natterson, M.D.
This book is not intended to replace the advice or treatment of health-care professionals. It should be considered an additional resource only. Questions and concerns about mental or physical health should always be discussed with a doctor or other health-care professional.

Library of Congress Cataloging-in-Publication Data

Is this normal? : more girls' questions, answered by the editors of The care & keeping of you / edited by Darcie Johnston ; illustrated by Josée Masse.—2nd edition.
    pages   cm
Audience: Ages 8+.
ISBN 978-1-60958-906-6 (pbk.)—ISBN 978-1-60958-948-6 (ebook)
1. Girls—Health and hygiene—Juvenile literature. 2. Grooming for girls—Juvenile literature. I. Johnston, Darcie, editor. II. Masse, Josée, illustrator.
RA777.25.I88 2015   613'.04242—dc23   2014024147

Main

A Letter to You

Millions of girls have read *The Care & Keeping of YOU*. Those readers have written us letter after letter about the way they look and the way they feel: Letters about hair and skin and teeth and nails. Letters about puberty and periods, breasts and bras. Letters about feelings and moods.

Some girls are worried they're growing up too fast. Others feel like they're being left behind. Most want to know if what they're going through is normal.

Whatever you're concerned about, you're sure to find letters in this book from girls who feel the same way you do. Reading the letters may feel like you're talking with good friends—girls like you. And we hope our responses will answer *your* questions, too.

If you want to know more after reading (and you probably will), ask your parents or another adult you trust. Read the "Tips for Talking with Parents" at the back of this book to get you started. You might feel embarrassed or nervous at first, but just jump in. Each conversation will be easier than the last and will help you feel more confident about the changes ahead.

Your friends at American Girl

Contents

Grooming & Hygiene 7
Letters from you about hair, shaving, acne, makeup, braces, glasses, nails, keeping clean, and more

Body Basics 35
Letters from you about breasts and bras, periods, pads and tampons, growth spurts, pubic hair, and more

Health & Body Image   77

Letters from you about sleep, food, exercise, height and weight, ideas of beauty, and more

Moods & Feelings   101

Letters from you about mood swings, privacy, losing your cool, crushes, tears, and more

Tips for Talking   111
with Parents

Seven tips to help you talk with the trusted adults in your life about the things most on your mind

Grooming & Hygiene

Letters about hair, skin, teeth, nails, and more

Hair

Dear American Girl,

How often do I have to wash my hair now that I'm in puberty? It does not look that greasy, so I don't know why I have to wash it every day. Also, it's really long, and it takes forever for me to wash.

Wondering

For most girls in puberty, keeping their hair clean means washing it several times a week, using a shampoo made for their hair type. But you don't need to shampoo every day unless your hair is very oily or you're very active or athletic. And you shouldn't shampoo every day if you have a sensitive or dry scalp. If washing your long hair is taking more time than you can give, this may be a great time to consider a shorter style. A shoulder-length cut has most of the advantages of long hair with less shower time.

I want long hair, but it doesn't look good after a while and I have to get it cut off. What can I do? I have to keep starting over.

Trying

I am trying to grow my hair long. My mom says it still needs to be trimmed, but I don't want to lose a single inch. Why does it need to be trimmed?

Wannabe Rapunzel

Although it may not make sense, hair needs to be trimmed while you're trying for those Rapunzel locks, because the ends of your hair naturally split and break off. Trimming removes these frizzy-looking ends and keeps hair healthy while it grows.

You can reduce split ends by being kind to your hair. Don't brush more than you need to. Use only a wide-tooth comb after shampooing because wet hair breaks more easily than dry hair, and comb gently. Use a conditioner or detangler to make combing easier, too. And last: Heat is hard on hair, so use a blow dryer on a low or cool setting and avoid curling or straightening irons.

Hair grows about half an inch a month, so if you trim a quarter inch every couple of months, your hair growth will far outpace the amount you trim. With care and patience, your hair will be long—and beautifully healthy.

Dear American Girl,

This summer AND the summer before, I got head lice. If I go through it one more time, I am going to go seriously crazy. This time my mom cut off my hair with scissors, and I cried and cried. How can I stop getting them??? It's HORRIBLE!

Sick of It

It's probably no surprise that head lice are very contagious! These tiny insects move fast, and they can live for a short time on a hat or hairbrush until they find a head of hair to call home. As a result, they can be spread when two heads touch, such as while playing or hugging, and when sharing things that touch hair. To lower your chance of catching lice again, never share hairbrushes, combs, hair ties, headbands, or any other accessory used in hair. Don't share your own, and don't borrow anyone else's. Watch out with hats, headphones, and pillows, too. Having short hair or wearing your hair up does not protect you, so follow these rules no matter what your hairstyle is.

Dear American Girl,

I am scared to wear shorts and skirts to school because I have such hairy legs. I am 11 years old. Is this the right age to start shaving, or should I wait a little longer?

Ready to Shave

Dark hairs on your legs are normal. Other girls your age are sprouting them, too, and some girls are starting to shave. If you feel ready to learn how to remove hair from your legs, let your parent know. Try saying, "I've been feeling really self-conscious about the hair on my legs and would like to know more about shaving." If your mom or dad thinks you're too young, don't be discouraged. Ask if you can talk about it again in a few months or when the weather gets warmer and it's time to break out the shorts.

Dear American Girl,

What is the difference between all the ways you can remove hair from your legs? So far I've heard of tweezing, depilatory, waxing, and bleaching. Are these better than shaving? My mom says I can start shaving, but I would like to know what the options are.

Full of Questions

Shaving is the way most girls and women remove hair from legs. You need to learn to use a razor carefully, because it's very sharp, but once you're good at it, shaving is easier than any of these other methods.

- Tweezing (or plucking) is pulling hairs out with tweezers, one at a time. Although it's a good way to remove a *few* hairs, trying this on your legs would take hours! It would also be painful.

- A depilatory is a chemical product that weakens hair. It's applied to the skin, it sits for several minutes (longer than it takes to shave), and then it's wiped off, taking the hair with it. This may sound simple, but it can irritate skin—and it's messy and smelly!

- Waxing is usually done by a professional, who spreads wax on an area of skin, then quickly yanks it off like a bandage, pulling the hairs out by the follicle. Like tweezing, it can hurt, and it can irritate skin. This method is usually used with smaller areas, not whole legs.

- Bleaching hair lightens its color instead of removing it. It's mainly used on fine hairs on the arms or face, not on legs. Like a depilatory, it can irritate skin, and if the hair or skin is naturally dark, bleaching may not accomplish the job.

 Don't try any method on your own. Before you try one that interests you—including shaving—talk with your mom or dad.

12

Dear American Girl,

I have tiny hairs on the top of my lip and it looks like I am growing a mustache. I was wondering if you had a solution to that.

No Stash

Visible hairs above the lip are not unusual once puberty has started, especially for girls with dark hair. The hairs are more noticeable to you than to anyone else, but if they really bother you, talk with your parent. Your mom can help you pluck the most visible hairs with tweezers. Once you get older, if you want to deal with more than a few hairs, a chemical hair remover or bleach made just for the face is a possibility. Both are available in drugstores, but they can burn your skin and must be used carefully and always with a parent—never on your own. Another option is professional waxing, which is effective but has an "ouch" factor. Every method has pros and cons. Start slow.

Dear American Girl,

I am 10 and I have super-hairy arms and legs. Some people make fun of me and I try to laugh with them, but it really does hurt.

Fuzzy

All people have hair everywhere on their bodies, ranging from fine to thick and from light to dark. It's normal and healthy. But if your body hair bothers you—and only you—you could try making some of your hair less noticeable. Talk with a parent about your feelings, and ask your doctor for any recommendations he or she might have for someone your age. As for the teasing, laughing along may help keep insensitive remarks from getting out of hand. But if you're feeling hurt, try leveling with these people, especially if they are your friends: "You probably don't mean to hurt my feelings, but it bothers me when you make fun of me. Please stop."

Face & Skin

Dear American Girl,

My skin is getting greasy. My mom had greasy skin and pimples when she was my age. Is there anything I can do to keep my skin from breaking out?

Grease Face

Oily skin isn't a bad thing. Without oil, your skin would feel dry and rough. But as you start puberty, your oil glands may start working overtime, clogging your pores and leading to breakouts. The best way to avoid breakouts is to care for your skin before they happen: Wash your face every morning and night with warm water and an oil-free cleanser, and follow up with an oil-free face lotion. Avoid pore-cleaning strips and toners—they're meant for adult skin. And don't wash your skin more than twice a day. If you strip your face of too much oil, your glands will work extra hard to give your skin back the oil it lost. To fight shine during the day, just blot your skin with clean facial tissues.

Dear American Girl,

I have TONS of pimples and blackheads on my face. What can you recommend?

Need Answers

To help get pimples under control, look for the ingredient *salicylic acid* or *benzoyl peroxide* on the label of an oil-free acne gel or cream. Benzoyl peroxide kills bacteria that can cause pimples, and salicylic acid mainly helps keep pores from clogging. To use either one, spread a small amount (about the size of a pea) evenly around your face after washing and drying it. Be careful to keep it away from your eyes and mouth—it's strong stuff. Use the product only two or three times a week to start, and work up to using it every day if your skin doesn't get too dry or irritated. Experiment to see which one works best for you. If your acne is more severe, try using them together, or use one in the morning and the other at night. If this doesn't help get your acne under control, talk to your parents about seeing your doctor. Treatments are available that can help even the most severe cases.

Dear American Girl,

I have pimples on my arms. I wash my arms, but they are still there. What should I do? Is this normal?

Getting Picked on by Pimples!

During puberty, many girls get small, skin-colored bumps on their upper arms or thighs. The bumps aren't pimples, although they may look like them. Instead, they're a harmless condition called *keratosis pilaris,* which just means "bumpy skin." To help them go away, try using a washcloth or loofah in the shower (gently—no hard scrubbing!), and then use an oil-free moisturizer. No matter what, the bumps will start to disappear as you get older.

Freckles and fair skin are part of who you are, along with your hair and eye color. Try letting your friends know you're OK with the features you were born with by saying, "I like my freckles" or "I think they're cool." It's true that you have no control over your freckles, but one thing you can—and should—control is your exposure to the sun, which can cause a different kind of freckles and sunburn, too. Use a sunblock with an SPF of 30 or higher, and stay out of the sun in the middle of the day to avoid damaging your fair skin. Wearing a hat with a brim that shades your face is also a good idea.

Dear American Girl,

I blush all the time, which is already embarrassing, but I have a friend who laughs at me whenever it happens, and that makes it 10 times worse. How can I stop blushing, and how can I get her to stop teasing me?

Red Face

Blushing is your body's way of reacting to stress. Some people sweat, some people shake, some people (like you) blush. And as you already know, when someone points out your blushing, it only makes your cheeks burn brighter. The next time your friend laughs, try saying, "I feel even more embarrassed when you point it out. I wish you wouldn't do that." Let her know that the friendliest thing she can do is ignore your flushed face and change the subject. That will give you a chance to cool your hot cheeks by taking lots of deep breaths or splashing them with cold water.

Dear American Girl,

I've been noticing stretch marks on my hips and at the top of my legs. My mom says I'm getting them because my skin is too dry. I put lotion on them, but they don't go away. Can you tell me how the stretch marks got there and how to make them disappear?

Streaks

Stretch marks happen when your body grows very quickly—such as during puberty. In fact, most girls (and boys) get them. Putting lotion on stretch marks might help dry skin feel more comfortable. However, the marks aren't caused by dry skin, and lotion won't make them disappear. Nothing can actually remove them, but their dark pink or purplish color will eventually fade to the color of your normal skin, and you'll hardly notice them.

Dear American Girl,

I have a birthmark on my face. My friends say it's my "uniqueness," but I can't believe them. When people notice it, it really bothers me.

Tired of It

It's normal for people to be curious about birthmarks. If they comment on yours, just say, "It's a birthmark. I was born with it." You may be wondering about ways you could cover it up or remove it altogether when you're older. But actually, you might find it hard to imagine your face without it—it really is part of what makes you unique. Trust your friends, who know what real beauty means, and remember their words when people's curiosity gets on your nerves.

Glasses & Contacts

Dear American Girl,

I'm 12 and I want to wear contacts instead of glasses, but my parents keep saying, "Maybe next prescription." I've been waiting for two years!

Responsible Enough

Are your parents worried about your health and safety? Contact lenses need to be cleaned and stored carefully to prevent eye infections. Show your parents that you're up to that task by being responsible with other hygiene habits. Brush and floss your teeth every day. Keep your hair combed. Take showers without being reminded. If your parents still think you're too young, ask them to talk with your eye doctor to get all the facts. Then relax, knowing that there's nothing more you can do but that you'll have those contacts one day soon.

Dear American Girl,

I am probably going to get glasses, and I really don't want to. My mom says I look good in glasses, but I don't!

Dreading Glasses

If you don't like the way you look in glasses, you probably haven't tried on enough styles. There are a ton of fun styles in all kinds of colors, ranging from cool blue to bubble gum pink to classy copper. Some frames are decorated with beads and gems, or swirls and stars. Some go for a more sporty look. Some are so thin you can barely tell they're on your face. Ask your parent if you can visit an eyeglass shop or two, and bring a friend along for another opinion.

When you're wearing your new glasses, take a look at the people around you. Lots of them will be in glasses, too, and they may be looking back at you, admiring *yours*!

Advice from Girls

"If you need to wear glasses, think of them as a cool fashion accessory. That's what I do, and I don't feel embarrassed to wear them."

—An American Girl, age 11

Sweating & Odor

Dear American Girl,

This year I have had a big problem: sweating. I can't help it, and when it happens it is very noticeable. I wear deodorant and I wash my underarms, but it never stops!

B.O. Queen

Everyone sweats—it's your body's way of keeping you cool. But when sweat mixes with bacteria, it causes a smell. Wash your underarms thoroughly with soap every day—and every time after you exercise. Then apply a deodorant with antiperspirant, which cuts down on the amount you sweat. Wear clean cotton clothes for gym class, and take them home afterward to wash. If you don't have time to shower after gym, wash your underarms with damp wipes and reapply deodorant.

Dear American Girl,

My feet sweat a LOT, even when I wear flip-flops, which makes them smell BAD!!! I have tried everything, but nothing works. I need some way to make them stop.

Sweaty Feet

Stinky feet are caused by sweat interacting with bacteria in your shoes. During puberty, the problem can be worse because hormones make you sweat more. The key to sweeter-smelling tootsies is keeping your feet clean and your shoes dry. Here are some tips to follow every day:

- Always wear clean, dry, absorbent socks when you wear shoes.

- Change your socks and shoes at least once a day. If you've worn a pair of socks, don't put them back on without washing them first.

- Wear shoes and sandals made out of materials that let your feet breathe, such as canvas, leather, or mesh. Avoid plastic or vinyl.

- Wash your feet every day with soap and warm water. Scrub thoroughly with a washcloth, and be sure to get between your toes.

- Make sure your feet are dry before putting on socks and shoes.

- Try dusting your tootsies with cornstarch baby powder to absorb dampness.

Makeup

There is no "right" age, but some girls start to wear a little makeup in middle school. Moms and dads often don't want girls starting earlier for reasons that have to do with your health and even your sense of who you are. For example, parents want their daughters to feel pretty *without* makeup first so they learn to use it the right way: to enhance their natural beauty instead of covering it up. Also, you should already have a habit of washing your face every morning and evening before adding makeup to your routine. You can respect your mom's rule and have fun talking together about the makeup you'll start wearing once you turn 12.

Dear American Girl,

I am 13, and my mom says I can start to wear makeup. I'm super excited, but what should I buy? Do you have any advice?

Don't Want to Look Fake

Start slowly with products that are natural looking, such as a clear pink lip gloss and clear or brown (not black) mascara. Powder or foundation on your face is for when you are older, but try an oil-free concealer on blemishes, dabbing it on the spot and then smoothing it gently with your finger. For special occasions, you might add a smudge of eye shadow in a color that's not too bright or dark. If you want to be bold, experiment with nail polish colors. Ask your mom or another adult for help choosing the right products to keep your skin healthy—the look of real beauty.

Dear American Girl,

I'm 13 and have the worst under-eye circles ever, no matter how much sleep I get. I usually put a concealer on them. Is there any way to get rid of them?

Hannah

If the skin under your eyes is thin or fair, it's easier to see the tiny blood vessels that create the look of dark circles. The problem can be made worse by lack of sleep, because this slows your circulation down, causing blood to pool in those tiny vessels around your eyes. Circles can also be caused by hay fever or other allergies, which cause the blood vessels to swell. Try to get at least nine hours of sleep every night. If you have allergies to pollen or pets, talk with your parent—and your doctor—about treatments, and keep pets out of your room. With your parent's help, you could also try a drugstore eye cream for circles. If you use a concealer, apply the eye cream first and let it dry. Then lightly dab on a liquid concealer that matches your skin color and gently blend it in.

Ear Piercing

Dear American Girl,

I have been asking Mom for a couple of years if I can get my ears pierced. Nearly all my friends have their ears pierced, and last year I was the only girl in my class who didn't. What do you think is a good age to get my ears pierced?

Ready for Earrings

Any age that both you and your mom are happy with is a good age. Prove to your mom that you're responsible and mature by respecting her decision. Don't keep bringing it up. Instead, show your mom how much pierced ears will mean to you by starting an earring collection or saving money to put toward the cost of the piercing. If it's all right with her, buy some stick-on or clip-on earrings, too, so that you can practice wearing them. When your mom sees how serious and excited you are, she may allow you to pierce your ears early. But if she doesn't, stay focused on the future. When your time comes, you'll have the money and the earrings ready to go.

Braces

Dear American Girl,

I'm getting braces. I'm scared I'll look like a dork and people will tease me. Also I won't be able to eat half of the things I eat now, and I don't want my mom to think I don't like what she is making if I can't eat it.

Scared of Braces

Many kids have braces. Braces are so common now that even lots of adults are wearing them, too. Your braces won't be the talk of the school. If you want to take attention off them, wear an interesting shirt or a sparkly hair accessory. Remember, though, that your best accessory is your smile. If you smile naturally and show off your braces, you won't have to worry about hiding them anymore. And you'll see that they're not the big deal you're imagining they'll be. As for your parents, just talk about your "can't eat" list. They'll be touched that you're concerned about their feelings.

**Still worried?
Here are some
reassuring words
from girls like you:**

"When I got braces, I was worried, too. But when I went to the first day of school, about half the school had braces! Nobody noticed mine. Just be yourself, and don't worry about your teeth."
—age 12

"Remember this: Kids all over America have braces. Next time you have an orthodontist appointment, ask for the cool colors for your bands so that you can express yourself."
—age 12

"Braces are cool! You get to change the colors of your bands and eat ice cream or pudding when you get them tightened. I have straight teeth, but I would love to have braces."
—age 13

"Don't fret! Tons of other girls in your grade will have braces. If someone hurts your feelings, tell some of the other girls with braces how you feel. They'll understand and be able to relate."
—age 10

"Once my friend came back to school with her braces OFF, and she got a lot of attention. We had to get used to her new look because we all thought braces looked so good on her."
—age 9

Nails

Dear American Girl,

I have hangnails. I have had them for a long time. I talked to a doctor, and she said to put lotion on them and then to put gloves over them so I don't touch them. I did it for a couple of days, and it has not worked. I don't know what else to do. Please help.

Sore Fingers

You're on the right track—you just need to stay on it. It might take a little while for your hangnails to get better. And if you're in the habit of picking at them, it will also take time to break that habit. Rub a mild moisturizing cream or petroleum jelly on them every morning and evening. You can wear lightweight, knit cotton gloves at night to avoid touching your fingers. During the day, try covering an especially bad hangnail with an adhesive bandage. Carry a pair of nail clippers with you, too, so that you can trim a hangnail instead of picking or tearing it off. When you feel the urge to touch your hangnails, rub them with your moisturizer instead of picking at them. Your fingers should be like new in a few weeks. If they ever look or feel really sore, though, let your parent know.

Dear American Girl,

I have a bad habit of biting my fingernails. My mom said if I go a month without biting them she will get me a new doll. How can I do it? Sometimes I don't even realize I'm doing it!

Nail-Biter

You said it: Habits like nail biting can be hard to break because we do them automatically. Before you've noticed, your finger is in your mouth and your teeth are at work. Give your hands something to do so they don't drift up to your mouth. Doodle on a pad of paper, squeeze a stress ball, or play cat's cradle with some string. Keep your mouth busy, too, by chewing on a piece of sugar-free gum during times when you would normally nibble your nails. Pack nail clippers or an emery board in your backpack so that if you chip a nail you won't try to fix it with your teeth. Paint your nails so they're too pretty to bite. And look for ways to reward yourself when you make it through the day without nibbling. Put a quarter in a piggy bank—and save up for clothes and accessories for your new doll!

Body Basics

Letters about breasts, periods, and other puberty stuff

Puberty

Dear American Girl,

I'm 12 years old and I feel like I'm growing way too fast. I have developed breasts and have already had my first period.
Early Bloomer

All of my friends have started their periods and have breasts. I'm nowhere close to having my period, and I'm already 12. My mom says I'll get my breasts and period eventually, but I feel so left out.
Late Bloomer

Sooner or later, everybody blooms. For girls, puberty usually starts between the ages of 8 and 13, and their first period can start anytime between 8 and 16. That's a pretty wide range, but it's all normal! Girls who start on the early side usually feel self-conscious about their developing bodies, while "late bloomers" often worry they'll never catch up. Even among girls who are the exact same age—like both of you—some feel they're too fast and others feel they're too slow. In fact, probably every girl feels either one way or the other, depending on where her friends are in the puberty process. Knowing all of this might help—you are not alone. The truth is, you're both right on time.

Dear American Girl,

I've had my pubic hair for almost two years, but my breasts haven't developed much yet and I still don't have my period. My mom said it's because I'm so small, but why does that matter? Is she right?

Confused

No two people go through puberty in exactly the same way. The first sign can be pubic hair, the beginnings of breasts, or increased sweating or moodiness. From there, it can take a couple years or longer to get all the way to having periods. In other words, your timing is normal. Body size and puberty are indeed related, but not in the way you might be thinking. It's simply that during puberty, kids gain several inches and pounds, and your body needs fuel (rather than size) for all that growth. If you're eating well, being small isn't keeping you from puberty. When your body decides it's time, you will start to grow. Just be sure to give it the fuel it needs by eating healthy foods in healthy amounts. Your body type may be naturally slight and shorter than average, and your breasts may not grow as full as others, but that's normal, too.

I have a friend who I know has started puberty, and I have, too. I want to be able to talk to her about it, but I don't want to make her feel awkward. She is the only other girl who has started puberty, though. So how do I start up a conversation without any awkwardness?

Can We Talk?

If she's already a friend, you're halfway there. Invite her to your home after school, or out for ice cream or a bike ride on the weekend. Away from school, you have the time and privacy you need to talk about personal things. The topic of puberty may just bubble up on its own. One of you has to break the ice, though, and it might need to be you. Tell her something about you, such as, "I've been wondering if it's time to get a bra, but I'm not sure how to bring it up with my mom" or "Do you think we're old enough to shave yet?" or "Sometimes I feel like crying and I don't even know why." Once you get started, you'll probably find that she's as happy as you are to have someone to talk to about all the changes you're going through. If your friend seems reluctant, though, move on to less personal topics. If she ever does want to talk about it, she'll know that she can come to you.

Dear American Girl,

My legs are always sore. And it doesn't help that I run and play a lot. I think it might be a growth spurt but I'm not sure. Help.

Always Sore

During puberty, you might grow as much as 3 or 4 inches taller in a single year! A lot of that growth is happening in your legs, and that can make them feel achy, crampy, or tired. This growth spurt will end about two years after you start your period, and so will the growing pains that go with it. To deal with the pains, try rubbing the area or using a heating pad or cold pack. If massage, heat, and cold don't help, ask your parent about a pain-relieving medication such as ibuprofen. And if a joint seems swollen or you feel sick—be sure to let your mom or dad know. It may be time to see a doctor.

Dear American Girl,

I'm scared to grow up. I like being a kid and playing with my friends. Do you get to play as a teenager???

Still a Kid

I'm going to go into puberty in about a year or two, and I am FREAKING out. I've talked to my mom and asked her every possible question, read every book on periods, and we're now learning about it at school. But somehow I still feel shaky. I want to be prepared! What to do?

Still Not Prepared

You're growing up, but you're still you. Puberty won't turn you into a different person, and you can keep doing all the things you enjoy. Also, it happens one thing at a time, over several years—not all at once. And your friends will be with you, sharing these experiences, plus you have parents, family members, teachers, and others to talk with when you're confused or scared. That said, you've read about puberty and heard about it, so you're prepared. It feels a little scary now only because you're not there yet, so you don't quite know what to expect. Everyone goes through puberty. You can, too. Remember that you've already been through some big changes in your life that felt scary at first, such as starting school, and you managed. Remind yourself, too, to talk with people who care about you when you need answers or reassurance. And have fun with your friends, laughing, playing, and being there for one another.

Breasts & Bras

Dear American Girl,

*I'm 8 years old, and I have breast buds. Am I too young?
I am really scared.*

V. from California

*I am 9 and I am getting bigger breasts than I used to have.
No one in my class has breasts. Am I growing too fast? This
doesn't seem right. I don't want to grow up yet.*

Growing Too Fast

Breasts are often the first sign that puberty is starting, and most girls
feel both happy and scared to discover them on their chest. Ask your
mom how old she was and how she felt when she started developing breasts. Chances are, she had many of the same concerns that
you do. Remember that this is only the beginning of a process that
will take many years. You won't wake up tomorrow with fully grown
breasts. Not only that, you don't have to suddenly act like a grown-up
either. You can still be a kid, and still do all the same things you used
to do. Even better, you might also be able to do some things that you
couldn't do a year or two ago. Focus on the good parts of growing up.
There are many more to come, in time.

Stage 1

This is how most breasts look before puberty begins. Breasts are flat to the chest, with a raised nipple and small areola.

Stage 2

A raised bump called a breast bud begins to develop under each nipple. The nipples and areolas get larger and darker. You may feel some tenderness in this area as the breasts grow.

Stage 3

The nipple and areola continue to grow and can get even darker in color. Breasts get larger and may look a bit pointy.

Stage 4

The areola and nipple blend together into a mound that rises above the breast. Some girls skip this stage.

Stage 5

Breasts are fully developed, with a rounder, fuller shape. The areola and nipple form a mound that rises above the breast. The nipple is raised above it.

Dear American Girl,

I really want breasts! How long is this going to take? All my friends have them. I want them to come now!!!

K.Q.

I own three regular bras and two sports bras, but I don't have breasts yet. I am 11, and every girl in my class is already wearing a bra. When are my breasts coming??

Anti-Bra Girl

Lots of girls feel impatient when their friends already have breasts—and just as many girls worry that their breasts are growing too soon or too fast. How quickly you develop has to do with your genetics and your weight. Some girls don't start until they're 12 or 13, but once they do, they catch up quickly. Check with your doctor to find out where you are on your developmental path. Then reassure yourself that one day you really, truly will have breasts.

Dear American Girl,

My breasts seem to be at different stages. One of my breasts is almost in the middle of Stage 2 but the other one is just beginning Stage 2. What happens if my breasts turn out lopsided?

Lopsided

When it comes to breasts, I have one big one and one flat one. When I put on a bathing suit, the big one puffs out. Even my friend said, "Wow, big and little one!" What can I do?

Too Different

Breasts take time—four or five years from when you first notice breast buds until they are fully formed. Along the way, one breast can grow at a different rate than the other. They will even out by the time you're grown, though. In the meantime, if one breast is noticeably larger, talk to your mom about getting a swimsuit with removable pads and try removing the pad from the side for the larger breast but leave the other pad in. You might also use a pad with your smaller breast in your bra if you feel self-conscious.

Dear American Girl,

I want to ask my mom about wearing a bra, but I'm afraid my breasts are too small and she'll say no.

Emma

I'm 8 years old. I think I'm in Stage 2. Do I need a bra? Do I have to wear it every day?

Need a Bra?

I'm almost 11 and some of my friends have already started to wear bras. I'd like one, too, but I'm not sure if it's time for me to wear them.

A.B.

Many girls start wearing a bra when their breasts are at Stage 2, but it may not be until Stage 3 that they wear one all the time or feel they really need one. Ask your mom if you can start with a training bra or a sports bra, both of which are made to fit every size girl. You could say, "I'd really like to get used to wearing a bra" or "I'd feel more comfortable wearing a bra." If your mom doesn't think you're ready, remember this: Bras are private matters. You can't always tell if a girl is wearing one, which means that other people can't tell whether you are—especially if you layer your shirts. If you feel self-conscious about not wearing a bra, try wearing a tank top or camisole with another shirt over the top.

Dear American Girl,

At my school we wear uniforms with a white shirt. My bra shows through my shirt, and my friends can see it. I feel really embarrassed.

TX Girl

When I got all of my bras, it was exciting to pick pretty colors and patterns. But now I regret it because they show through my shirts!

N.K. from L.A.

Even white bras can show through light-colored tops. Try wearing a bra that matches your skin tone. If you can see the bra through your shirt—especially if it's a uniform and you don't have the choice to change it—layer a tank top or camisole over the bra. Some tank tops have breast support built in, so you can skip your bra and get a smooth look beneath your shirt. If the wires or seams of your bra show through your clothing, try a seamless bra or a sports bra. You might also consider getting a bigger uniform or wearing larger tops. The tighter your shirt, the more likely it is to show every seam, hook, and wire.

Training bras are perfect for girls whose breasts don't fit the standard cup sizes yet (such as A, B, and C). If you've developed past the breast bud stage, a sports bra is as good a choice as a cup bra. A sports bra may seem less obvious than a cup bra, and it will give your breasts plenty of support. You may feel awkward being the first among your friends to move beyond a training bra, but you'll probably feel more comfortable with a bra that supports—and your friends will quickly catch up.

It's easy to confuse padded bras and cup bras, but they are not the same thing. Padded bras are a style of cup bra with extra material that adds size and coverage. But padding is not necessary for support, and you can find cup and sports bras without it. The most important consideration is having a bra that fits right, so it's a good idea to be measured by a salesperson in a lingerie shop or section of a department store to find out your size. Ask your mom if you can go shopping together and get measured. You'll be able to choose a bra that's comfortable for you and has the Mom Seal of Approval.

Dear American Girl,

I have some bras, but they are so uncomfortable. How can I get used to them?

So Uncomfortable

I want to wear my bras, but they bother me. I guess I need to know what kind of bra would feel better.

Uncomfy Girl

My mom said I should wear a bralet, but they feel itchy. What should I do?

Chloe

Bras do take some getting used to. The good news is that they come in different styles and fabrics. The bra you're wearing may not be a good fit for you. Ask your mom if you can go shopping for a more comfortable style. Try a soft-cup bra, one without underwire. Or look for one made with spandex, a stretchy material that moves with your body. Ask a sales associate at the store to bring you styles she thinks might be most comfortable, and keep trying them until you find one that feels good.

Dear American Girl,

What I'm worried about is my nipples. Sometimes they are pointy, and other times they are sort of flat on my breast. Is this something to be concerned about?

Worried 'Bout the Buds!

Breast nipples have lots of nerves in them. This makes them sensitive to touch and temperature. If your shirt rubs against your nipples, for example, or if you get cold, those nerves can "wake up" and cause the muscles around them to tense up. When that happens, your nipples become hard and pointy—until the nerves calm back down. Even certain thoughts and feelings, such as being excited, can wake up the nerves. While all this is normal, it often bothers kids that their bodies are doing something whether they like it or not. (This happens to boys' nipples, too!) Girls, especially, might find it annoying because they worry that other people can see the hard nipples through their shirt. Wearing a bra and a shirt or sweater that doesn't fit tightly should help.

Pubic Hair

Dear American Girl,

I am only 10 years old, and I've started to grow pubic hair. My mom was 13 when hers started growing. Am I growing too fast?

K.

Every girl develops on her own time and in her own order when it comes to the signs of puberty. Age 10 is perfectly normal for pubic hair to start growing. Girls sometimes start puberty around the same time as their moms— but not always. In fact, the age when girls are starting puberty has been getting younger since your mom was a girl. At your next checkup, your doctor will check your development and make sure you're growing right on schedule.

Dear American Girl,

I have pubic hair. I'm the first one of my friends to have it. Whenever we change for gym class, I can see my friends looking down and laughing at me. I've told my mom, and she said they'll all get it soon. But it makes me feel bad, and I want it to stop.

Embarrassed

When you're changing clothes in gym, try not to wonder if others are looking at you. Act confident, even if you don't feel that way. And if one of your friends laughs, you might look her in the eye and say, "What are you laughing at? We're all growing up, you know!" or "Hey, please don't laugh at me. It's hard enough being 10 (or 9 or 11...)!" Your mom is right: Your friends will be changing soon, too. In fact, they may be laughing because they're anxious about that very thing. When it starts to happen, the teasing will stop.

Dear American Girl,

I have pubic hair and I love to swim. How can I wear a swimsuit without hair sticking out?

Longing to Swim

You might be able to cover your pubic hair with your swimsuit bottoms. If some hair shows, try wearing a suit with a skirt or ruffle at the bottom, or a "boy-cut" or "hipster" with bottoms cut low across the thigh. These suit styles hide hair better than bikini bottoms or other regular leg cuts. But if you really want to wear a bikini or you're worried about your hair showing no matter what suit you wear, you might consider shaving the edges of your pubic hair. Shaving there is tricky, because girls can get ingrown hairs when the hair is growing back, or the new growth can be extremely itchy. If you think you might want to shave, talk to a parent first and, at least the first time, don't shave your bikini area on your own.

Periods

Dear American Girl,

I am so nervous about starting my period. Every time I use the restroom I look at my pee to see if I did. I'm just really scared and am not sure I can do it.

Nervous

Thinking about something before it happens is sometimes a lot scarier than the actual thing when it does happen. You can ease some of your worry by being prepared ahead of time with pads at home and in your backpack. It might also be reassuring to think about your period as just another natural body process. In some ways, it's not so different from other body processes, such as breathing or sleeping or digesting food. Our bodies are made to do these things, they know how to do them automatically, and they've been doing them for a long, long time. Your body will do fine when it's time.

55

Dear American Girl,

Question #1: I'm not sure how to tell my mom when I get my first period. Any advice?

Question #2: How do I ask my mom to help me make a "First-Period Kit"?

Getting Ready

Talking with a parent about such private matters as your period can feel embarrassing or awkward. Remember that your mom has been through it, too, and she remembers her own nervousness. She's probably waiting for you to bring it up when you feel the time is right. Try saying, "Mom, I might be getting my period this year, so I was wondering if we could buy supplies so I'm ready?" You and your mom can put together a first-period kit for your school backpack that includes a pad or two, a change of underwear, and wet wipes in a small makeup bag or new pencil pouch. At home, have a box of pads on hand. Then, when your period does start, you'll have the supplies you need—and you'll be more comfortable (and maybe even excited!) telling your mom, since you've already been talking about it.

Dear American Girl,

I'm wondering how much blood to expect. Should I start wearing pads every day just in case I have a surprise period? How fast does the blood come? Will I have time to put on a pad without making a mess if I wasn't already wearing one?

Curious

I am really scared to get my period. The idea of blood loss from that area is just scary. What can I do to conquer my fears?

Scared

Until now, you've probably always thought of blood as something that has to do with getting hurt—like a cut or a scraped knee. Menstrual blood isn't like that. It's not part of a problem or an injury. Instead, it's a step in your normal, healthy development. And the total amount of blood during a period is only about 3 tablespoons. Try measuring out that much water into a cup; you will probably feel relieved when you see how little 3 tablespoons is. Also, the blood trickles out of your vagina over the course of several days, a small amount at a time. Especially with the first few periods, the flow can be even lighter, and it may begin as only a few drops. So you can relax. Just take note if there's a new feeling of moisture in your underpants, and check it out in the bathroom when you can. If you have a period kit in your backpack with a pad and a change of underpants, you're all set.

Dear American Girl,

I haven't started my period yet. What if I get it in school and I don't have a pad? Should I tell a teacher with a note or just in person? I'm freaking out!

Red Face

You'll feel much better if you take a few practical steps to get ready for your period. Whether you've had your first one or not, always keep a small zipper bag or other pouch with a couple of pads in the bottom of your backpack. That way you won't have to face the embarrassment of asking for one. If you do need to ask, though, tell yourself that this happens all the time. Your teacher may have supplies. Or even better, ask your school nurse, who almost certainly has anything you need—including reassurance—on hand.

Girls often wonder if their period will hurt, but there's no need to be afraid of pain every month. Many girls have no cramps at all. Some girls have sensations that range from small twinges to more noticeable cramps that last more than a day. If you're a girl who gets cramps, there are medicines such as ibuprofen that stop the discomfort—talk to your parents or doctor to find the dose that's right for you. A heating pad, a hot bath before or after school, and stay-ing active during the day also help. You might feel like sitting out of gym class, but moving your body will actually help ease period cramps. Just keep trying different things. You'll learn what makes your body feel better, and you'll see that your period doesn't have to "cramp" your style.

Dear American Girl,

I think I'm getting close to starting my first period. When I go to the bathroom, I see whitish sticky stuff on my underwear. I'm scared to ask my mom if it's starting.

Mc.B.

I'm almost 12 and my breasts have started growing. I read that two years after this you should have your period. Are there other signs it's coming?

Period at 13?

I have had a clear discharge for over two years, and still don't have my period. Is something wrong with me?

Almost 12

I am 11 years old and I haven't gotten my period yet. I've had vaginal discharge for a month, and I have breasts and pubic hair. I feel like my period could come at any moment and take me by surprise. I feel like I'm in the eye of a hurricane, awaiting the storm!

Emma

Sometimes I have cramps near my hips or belly. I haven't gotten my period yet, but does this mean it's coming? Just wondering.

Jacey

The time between the first signs of puberty and the arrival of your period is hard to predict. Most girls get their period anywhere between two and four years after they notice pubic hair or breast buds, but more time—or less—is normal, too. In any case, it happens toward the end of the puberty process, so you don't need to start planning for it until some of the other changes have started to appear, such as breast development, pubic hair, and vaginal discharge.

The discharge, which should leave a whitish patch in your underwear but not itch or burn, means your vagina and uterus are maturing. Any cramps you feel around your hips might mean your period is on its way—but they could also just be everyday twinges that you haven't noticed before. Now that you're paying more attention to what's going on with your body, you're more aware of what's happening on the inside as well as the outside.

Although it's not always true, girls often get their period around the same age as their mother. Ask your mom when she started and if she remembers any signs she had that it was coming. Besides maybe helping you predict your own period, talking about her experience can be fun for both of you and can open the door to more talks about whatever is on your mind.

How will I know if I did or didn't have my period yet? Can your period be light brown? I had some light brown for a few days, and then it stopped. Was that a period?

Wondering

I think I had my period, but it lasted only two days and there wasn't very much blood. Was that it?

Haley

Congratulations! Yes, that was your period. The first period is often short, with a small amount of blood, and the blood can be light or dark brown, rust-colored, pinkish, or red. You might find just a dry stain in your pad instead of actual liquid. And the blood might come and go—a little today, none tomorrow, more the next day. It's as if your body is practicing having a period, and your first few might be like this. Over time, as your periods become more established, expect them to become heavier and last longer.

Dear American Girl,

I'm 8 years old, and my parents are divorced. I live with my dad, and I'm embarrassed to tell him about my period when I get it. What should I do?

D.S.

Dads are pretty knowledgeable about periods. Chances are, your dad has thought about this and is waiting for you to bring it up whenever you're ready. You will feel better if you talk with him about this worry before your period starts—and how you'll handle it when it does start. Just getting the conversation going is the hardest part. Once you do, though, you'll probably find it's much easier than you thought. You could write him a note that says you've got something on your mind that's been hard to raise. He can then take the lead. This could also lead to more conversations about other ways your dad can support you after you get your period. Being open with him is a great way to let him know that you love and trust him. And talking with your dad now will make it easier to share other things with him in the future.

Dear American Girl,

I got my period about a year ago. At first everything was fine. I had to change my pads every two to four hours. But now my periods are really heavy, and I have to change every hour. Could there be something wrong?

Katy

First periods are often light and short. As a girl's hormones get established, her periods will usually get heavier and last longer. The blood will be more red than brown, and the periods will normally come every three to five weeks. It's not uncommon for a day or two at the beginning of a period to be pretty heavy. If you need help managing these heavy days, ask your parent for supplies labeled "maxi," "super," or "overnight." But if you're changing your pad every hour, or if your flow is heavy for several days, or if you keep getting your period every couple of weeks, let your mom or dad know so they can schedule a visit with your doctor. If you're bleeding too heavily, your body may not be able to make new blood cells quickly enough to replace them—a condition called *anemia* that's very easy to test for and treat.

Dear American Girl,

What are the signs that your period is a few days away?

Your Reader

Once you start having regular periods, you'll usually be able to tell that your period is about to start. Your breasts may feel tender. You may feel some cramping in your abdomen or back. Your body may feel heavier, or you may be more prone to breakouts. Over time, you'll learn the signals that your own body is giving you. One of the benefits of regular periods is that they come at about the same interval. Use a calendar to keep track of the first day of each period. After several months, you may start to see a pattern. For example, you might notice that your period starts about every four weeks, or maybe every 31 or 32 days. By charting them like this, you'll have another way of anticipating the next one.

Dear American Girl,

When I'm having my period and I'm at school, I feel like every single person can smell me. Mom says they can't, but I'm just not comfortable. I'm worried they can.

A.R.

Girls often worry about period odor, but your mom is probably right. If you change your pad or tampon regularly—every two to four hours—people should not be able to smell anything. Bathe or shower every day that you're having your period, too, making sure to wash well between your legs. "Scented" pads are available, but the perfumes in them can irritate your skin and are not necessary for stopping odor. Soap and water are all you need.

You may think you're one of the first girls in your class to get your period, so it's understandable that you feel self-conscious. Others will be starting their period soon, if they haven't already, so you won't feel singled out for long. In the meantime, to maintain your privacy, keep your supplies in a small pouch that you can easily carry in a pocket into the bathroom. If you're concerned about the sounds of opening up a pad or placing a used one in a bin, you can try to change pads when there are either no girls in the bathroom or several girls talking and running water—their noises will mask your own. However, it's probably best to put your energy into trying not to worry instead of trying to avoid discovery. If someone does figure it out, things will go better if you're prepared. Try not to show you're concerned, but be matter-of-fact and say something like, "Yeah, I started my period. I guess that will be happening to all of us soon" or "No big deal. I have my period. Just part of being a girl."

Period Products

Dear American Girl,

What kind of pads and tampons would you suggest for starters?

Want to Be Ready

When I start my period, what do you think I should use?

So Many Choices

Most girls start with pads. Because your first periods will probably be light, a package labeled "regular" should be fine. You may also want "panty liners" or "panty shields," which are ideal for when there's almost no flow. When your periods become heavier, you'll probably need some "maxi" or "super" pads, which can hold more blood. All pads have a sticky strip that attaches to your underpants, and some have extra strips called "wings" that wrap around the edges of your panties for even more coverage. If you decide you're ready to try tampons, look for the smallest size, which will be called "junior," "slim," or "slender." Most tampons come with an *applicator* to help you place the tampon inside the vagina. Tampons are also available without an applicator; many girls like their tiny size and find them easier to use. Whether you're buying pads or tampons, look for "unscented" on the label. Scented products can irritate the area around your vagina.

Dear American Girl,

Which one will be best for us—tampons or pads? We play soccer and do gymnastics. We're nervous about tampons.

S. and K., 7th Grade

I want to go to the pool and swim during my period. Do I have to use a tampon?

Scaredy Cat

Pads are fine during most sports, especially if you use a thin pad with wings. Wanting to play doesn't mean you have to start wearing tampons. Many girls do make the switch to tampons for athletics, though. With a lot of physical activity, they find tampons more comfortable, or when wearing a leotard they feel less self-conscious. One activity that does require tampons is swimming, since pads aren't designed to be in the water. If you're not ready to try tampons, just wear a pair of shorts at the pool or the beach and have fun doing other things besides swimming.

69

Dear American Girl,

I have some questions about tampons. Can you tell me how is the easiest way to put them in?

Samantha

I have no idea how you get the tampon string into the vagina. No idea!!!

J.G. from Dallas

uterus
vagina
tampon
applicator

1. Get Ready

Wash your hands, then unwrap the tampon. With one hand, find the labia at the opening of the vagina and use your fingers to spread the sides apart. With your other hand, hold the applicator at the bottom of the larger tube with your thumb and middle finger; place your index finger at the bottom of the narrower tube.

2. Insert

Insert the tip of the applicator into your vagina. Aim at a slight upward angle toward your back, and guide the large tube part of the applicator all the way into your vagina. Then push on the narrow tube with your index finger. This will push the tampon out of the applicator and into your vagina. Pull out the applicator and throw it away.

Based on the look of tampons and how to use them, it seems painful and complicated. But I really want to try. Do you have any tips?

Arizona

If you feel ready for tampons, first try experimenting. Plastic applicators glide better than cardboard and may be easier for beginners. Also, you might want to take a tampon out of its applicator to see what it looks like, then put it in a cup of water to see how it soaks up liquid. (Then throw it away.) Talk with your mom before you start, and read the directions on the box. Once you've done it a few times, you'll be a pro!

3. Check Fit

The string should now hang down between your thighs—it should not be inside the vagina. You won't be able to feel the tampon if it's in the right position. If it feels uncomfortable, though, it may not be in far enough. Use your finger to gently push it in farther. Wash your hands afterward.

4. Removal

When it's time to take out the tampon—within four to six hours—sit on the toilet, relax your muscles, and pull firmly on the string. The tampon will slide out. Don't flush the tampon down the toilet—this can clog drains. Instead, wrap it in toilet paper and throw it away. Wash your hands.

Dear American Girl,

My mom just got me tampons. I am really scared that I will accidentally get toxic shock syndrome. I also don't think I am ready for tampons.

Afraid

First, you don't need to use tampons—not now, not ever. A pad is always a good choice. A girl might consider a tampon when she feels comfortable with the idea of putting something in her vagina, which takes time getting used to, and when she can keep track of how long the tampon has been there. Toxic shock syndrome—or TSS—is a dangerous infection that can happen if a tampon has been left in the vagina for too long. It's very rare, but to be safe and to make sure they don't get it, girls and women are told to always remove a tampon within four to six hours. Just let your mom know that you appreciate the tampons and might want to try them sometime, but for now pads are perfect for you.

Dear American Girl,

What do I wear when I have my period and take a shower? **???**

Although it's fine to wear a tampon while you're in the shower or tub, you don't need to wear anything. Remember that your flow is not like a faucet that's been turned on. Some menstrual blood may trickle out, if it flows at all, but you can rinse it off while you're washing between your legs. Then just have a clean pad or tampon ready for when you're finished.

Vagina

A little bit of clear or whitish discharge is natural and healthy. It's your vagina's way of keeping itself clean. When girls start getting this discharge, though, it can be hard to get used to the new, damp feeling. One thing you can do is wear underpants made of cotton or that have a cotton lining. The cotton lets moisture pass through and evaporate, so your pants won't feel so wet. You can also try panty liners, which are too thin to feel in your underpants. Over time, the wet sensation will bother you less.

Dear American Girl,

It has been itching really badly in my period place. I don't feel comfortable scratching there in school and public. I do not know if there is a special cream I could get or anything I could do about it.

Gotta Scratch

Intense itching means that you could have a vaginal infection. Some infections are caused by different kinds of bacteria, but the most common is caused by a fungus known as *yeast*. A few yeast are normally in your vagina, but under the right conditions they can grow out of control. They really like hot, dark, damp places, for example, so avoid wearing sweaty exercise clothes, a wet bathing suit, or tight-fitting pants or underwear for too long. Most vaginal infections have similar signs—itching, soreness, and a discharge that's different from normal. Because they all have similar signs, it can be hard to tell whether an infection is yeast or something else. Tell your parents about the itching so that you can see a doctor. Your doctor will quickly find out what's causing the infection and give you the right medicine to treat it.

Health & Body Image

Letters about sleep, food, size, beauty, and more

Sleep

Dear American Girl,

I have trouble sleeping. I'm not scared or worried.
I just can't sleep, so I'm always sleepy. What can I do?

Sleepless in Texas

It takes me a long time to get to sleep at night. My
parents and I have tried everything from reading
stories to snuggling to lotion to journals to talking
to soaking baths. What more advice do you have?

Need Ideas

I can't fall asleep. No matter how much I try to relax,
I don't go to sleep until 10:00 or even later. Do you
have any advice?

Want to Zzzzzz

I get really uncomfortable at night and have a hard
time going to sleep.

Fidgety

 Here are some things you can do to help yourself get to sleep at night.

- Get plenty of exercise during the day. Exercise makes your brain work better in every way, including sleeping.
- No caffeine—that means chocolate and many drinks—in the evening.
- Start winding down with calming or relaxing activities two hours before bedtime.
- Have a bedtime routine. A set of steps you repeat every night tells your brain that it's time to get sleepy.
- Keep pets out of your room when the lights go out.

Once you're in bed, deep breathing and relaxation can help you fall asleep. Look for online demonstrations with your parents, and try relaxation CDs made specifically to help you fall asleep. Even without these tools, though, you can easily learn deep breathing. When you're in bed and in a comfortable sleep position, breathe in slowly through your nose, making sure your tummy expands (your mom or dad can practice this part with you). Hold the breath for a few seconds, then slowly breathe out. At the same time, picture in your mind a favorite comfortable place or thing, such as a quiet beach or a soft, sleepy puppy. Listening to a comforting audiobook might also help; audiobooks are more effective than soothing music as kids get older. A good night's sleep is important for feeling happy, staying healthy, and doing well in school, so if you're still not sleeping well, talk with your doctor for more ideas.

Dear American Girl,

I can't ever sleep because I'm not tired. I always get up and watch TV. I also get up and turn my light on. Is that OK? My mom worries that it's not good for my brain.

Lights On

Bright lights from electronic screens such as TVs, computers, tablets, and smartphones tell your brain, "Wake up!" Make a deal with yourself to turn them off at least an hour before bedtime and resist turning them back on if you wake up during the night. You'll be sleeping better soon. On the other hand, reading a print book or magazine before bed with a *soft* light can help to quiet the brain and get you ready to sleep. It won't wake you up the same way an electronic screen will.

Dear American Girl,

I've read that if you're trying to go to sleep, drinking milk can help. But what if you're really hungry? That's what happens to me a lot.

A.R.

If you're hungry before going to bed, talk with your mom or dad about an appropriate bedtime snack for you. It's not a good idea to eat a meal or big snack near bedtime, but a light snack is fine. Good choices are healthy, not too filling, and not spicy, and they don't contain caffeine. A small bowl of a whole-grain, minimally sweetened cereal—with milk—is ideal, because the combination might actually boost brain chemicals that help with relaxation and sleep.

Dear American Girl,

I still wet my bed. I am 9 years old. It's hard to go to sleepovers and camp. What should I do?

Embarrassing to Wet

I am almost 10 and I am still wetting the bed. I have tried everything but nothing is working. Any advice?

Bed Wetter :(

Bedwetting—also called *enuresis*—is more common than you think. It's usually caused when the brain doesn't wake you up when your bladder is full. It can also be caused by a urinary tract infection or other physical condition, so your first step is to visit your doctor to rule out that possibility. Once you're cleared of a physical problem, talk with your doctor about solutions, which might include a schedule of your parents waking you in the middle of the night to use the bathroom or an enuresis alarm. Your doctor might also give you medicine that can help during a sleepover or overnight camp. The good news is that no matter what, you will outgrow this problem one day and your nights will be dry.

Food & Nutrition

Dear American Girl,

Sometimes my friends forget that I'm a vegetarian. This makes it awkward when I go to dinner at one of their houses. They feel bad when they eat meat around me. How can I remind my friends that I don't eat meat but it's OK if they do?

Veggie Girl

Remind your friends that you're a vegetarian before you go to their house for a meal. Ask if they'd like you to bring your own main course—or pack a peanut butter sandwich just in case. If they offer you something with meat, politely skip the dish. Don't turn up your nose or say "Eww!" Just say as sincerely as you can, "That looks good," and then pass the dish to the next person. Fill up with an extra helping of something meatless. If you don't make a big deal out of what you do and don't eat, your friends won't either.

I'm a bit of a picky eater. I'm nervous that if I go to a friend's house or restaurant I've never been to before, there might not be anything that I like.

Too Picky

You can check out restaurant menus online or call ahead to see if there's something you like. And your friends (and their parents) might be aware of your picky palate and try to serve something they think you'll like. But this might be a good time for you to try being more adventurous. Go with your parents to the grocery store, and challenge yourself to choose something new each week. Help to prepare the foods, and try a few bites. You're bound to like some foods that you were pretty sure you wouldn't, which may make you feel braver about sampling things at a friend's house. If you don't like something your friend's parents serve, don't make a big deal out of it. Have another serving of something you do like. And remember that your tastes will change with time. There will be fewer foods that you haven't tried and many more that you love.

Dear American Girl,

I really like chips and cookies. They are my favorite snacks. I know they are junk food and they're bad for you, but I don't understand what the problem is. I am not overweight, so what's wrong with eating them?

Chip Lover

Everyone eats junk food, or food with little nutritional value, now and then. A little bit from time to time is OK. The problem is that you can fill up on junk food and not feel hungry, but you haven't given your body the nutrients it needs to grow and stay healthy. Substitute healthier snacks when you can, such as a piece of fruit, a handful of nuts or granola, a cup of yogurt, baby carrots and hummus dip, popcorn, or a slice of whole-grain bread with jam or peanut butter. If snacks like these aren't on hand in your home, ask your parents if they could add them to the shopping list.

Dear American Girl,

It makes me sad that I can't eat anything with gluten. I have celiac and have to bring my own food to parties and sleepovers. I also miss out on ordering lunch at school. It's sort of embarrassing. What do I do?

No Gluten

I have a peanut allergy, and I get hives when I eat peanuts. I feel as if my allergy is taking over what I eat!

Can't Eat Peanuts

You're not alone. Millions of kids in America have food allergies or other conditions that affect what they can eat. You've probably gotten smart about reading labels and carrying anything with you that you need, such as medicine or your own utensils. To keep from feeling left out of the fun, though, try getting creative about the things you *can* eat. If you have a peanut allergy, try a CC&J (cream cheese and jelly) sandwich instead of PB&J, or go in a different direction with hummus and crackers. If you have celiac disease, ask your parents to help you bake your own gluten-free cookies, and ask if you can shop with them. The number of tasty gluten-free foods is increasing all the time. Whether it's an allergy, celiac, or another dietary concern, always carry a safe snack with you. Visit health food stores, too, which may have special versions of your favorite foods. Want more support from friends? Teach them which foods you can't eat and what happens if you do. You could even educate your whole class by doing a science project. Show them, and yourself, that you control your food—it doesn't control you.

Dear American Girl,

How can I eat vegetables even though I don't like them? I only eat salad!!!! My mom keeps trying to get me to eat them. I know they are important if you want to be healthy and beautiful.

Trying

Eating a range of nutritious foods not only keeps your body healthy and your mind sharp, it also helps you feel happier and more energetic. Try adding small amounts of different veggies to the salads you already like: a handful of arugula or spinach leaves, shredded carrots, a cherry tomato, a slice or two of anything that looks interesting to you. Go for a colorful mix, and top it off with a favorite dressing—or try new dressing recipes. You might also like raw veggies with good-for-you dips, such as baby carrots with peanut butter or bell pepper strips with hummus. And talk with your parents about ways to sneak veggies into foods that you enjoy. Can you layer them under the cheese on pizza? Simmer them in pasta sauce? Bake them into breads or muffins? Get creative and be open to experimenting. But don't force yourself to eat anything that you truly don't like. There are plenty of good-tasting healthy foods out there. If you haven't found the ones you love yet, just keep looking!

Dear American Girl,

My best friend hardly eats anymore. At restaurants, she just orders a diet soda. At her house, she doesn't eat nearly as much as she used to. She always says that she weighs too much, but she doesn't. I'm worried that she might have an eating disorder.

Fearful Friend

You're right to worry. Eating disorders such as *anorexia* and *bulimia* can be very dangerous. A person with anorexia eats very small amounts of food and thinks she's overweight when she isn't—she's either very underweight or on her way there. She may also exercise much more than she needs to. With bulimia, a person may be normal weight, but she may overeat and then try to make up for it by throwing up or emptying the food from her body with laxatives. If your friend is still at a healthy weight, she may be in the early stages of an eating disorder, or there may be something else going on. Tell an adult about your fears. Talk to your parents, a teacher, or a school counselor who can check things out with your friend. If your friend finds out that you told someone, she may be upset with you, but be patient. In time, she'll see that speaking up was your way of showing her how much you care.

Does This Sound Like You?

If you think you might have anorexia or bulimia, don't try to deal with it all by yourself. Talk to an adult you trust—a parent, a teacher, a school counselor, or a doctor. Eating disorders can quickly take control of your life. The best way to fight back is to reach out for help.

Sports & Exercise

You're right: TV can be like an addiction. The first step for breaking the spell is to keep the TV turned off so that it can't pull you in. Don't turn it on when you get home from school or when you wake up on weekends. Don't drift toward it when someone else has it on. Just say no. You might decide on a couple of shows that you'd like to watch, and schedule those into your week. The trick, though, is to plan for those must-see programs in advance, then turn off the box as soon as they're over. If your parents keep the TV on all the time, talk to them about changing this habit. And if there's a TV in your bedroom, ask your parents to find another spot for it. The second step is diving in to all the great things you'll have time to do now. Like running. And dancing, biking, swimming, and soccer or some other sport—with or without a friend or a team. Soon you'll get such a good feeling from moving your body that your TV habit will be under control— and not controlling you.

Dear American Girl,

I'm not good at sports. In gym when we play games, I try to catch the ball. But when I fail, the kids on my team get mad at me. They also get mad when I do nothing. So what am I supposed to do?

Not a Sports Girl

It's hard to make the catch when you're worried about how your teammates will react. Tune them out by turning up the voice in your own head. Tell yourself, "I can catch the ball. I will catch the ball. That ball's *mine*." Picture yourself catching the ball, and imagine the feel of the ball in your hands. Spend time at home bouncing, kicking, and catching different balls so that ball play starts feeling more natural—and fun! And remember that you don't have to be a star athlete to be a good sport. Praise other players who try hard, even when they don't succeed. Praise yourself, too, for the things you did well or improved on. If your teammates see that you're trying your best, they'll go easier on you. They'll want you around for your positive spirit, and that positive spirit will help you play better, too.

Advice from Girls

"I do gymnastics, and I'm not as advanced as everyone else. I just remind myself of how far I've come since I started. Believe that you will get better. Work hard, and you will!"

—An American Girl, age 12

I have a problem. I need to get more active, but I don't like working out.

Couch Potato

Working out shouldn't feel like work. Focus on the fun ways you're already moving your body. Do you dance when you hear a song you love? That counts. Do you ride your bike to go visit a friend? That counts, too. Think about ways to add short bursts of activity throughout the day, such as chasing your dog in the backyard, taking stairs instead of the elevator, or playing tag at recess. Make up a new dance with a friend, or set up an obstacle course and time each other racing through it. Gather friends and record your own workout video. Wear crazy outfits and make up goofy routines. When you play it back, you'll work your stomach muscles—laughing! What's not to like about that?

"Too Small"

Dear American Girl,

I'm really skinny and short for 11 years old. The doctor says I'm fine. All the girls in my class call me Skinny Chicken, and it's so annoying.

Annoyed and Frustrated

I have always been the smallest in my class. I am super tired of everyone calling me "little girl." They don't know that I am probably older than THEY are!

NOT Little

The basic shape of your body is something you're born with. It's hard to be among the tallest or the smallest because of the attention that comes with that. You will fill out some and grow taller over the next few years, and one day the teasing will stop, no matter how slight you are. For now, though, you can embrace your body by getting involved in sports or other activities that make you feel and look strong. And when you're called names, look those kids in the eye and say something like, "I don't like it when you call me Skinny Chicken. I'm sure you don't mean to hurt my feelings, but it does hurt" or "I'm actually not a little girl. I'm probably older than you are! Plus, I like to think of myself as petite, not little."

"Too Big"

Dear American Girl,

I'm going into fifth grade and I'm overweight. I tried diets and not eating and meds, but nothing works, so what should I do?

K.M.

I weigh too much. I have been skipping breakfast and eating only a little at lunch and dinner, and I diet and exercise so I'll fit in at my new school.

Can't Win at Losing

I am fat. All of my friends say I'm not, but my doctor says I need to lose weight. It's hard to lose weight, and I'm having trouble doing that.

Someone Who Does Not Want to Be Named

I am 10 years old, and between my breasts and my belly I am large. I have tried eating right and exercising often, but it is never fun. Do you have any tips on making healthy lifestyles fun?

Alabama Gal

Eating nutritious foods, getting enough exercise, and maintaining a healthy weight help girls feel their best—both physically and emotionally. If your doctor says you weigh too much, work together and with your parents to set up a healthy eating and exercise plan. Your plan might include a nutritionist. It should include a sport or physical activity that you enjoy. No matter what, you'll want to have support from trusted adults to help you stick with the plan.

A complete plan works. Most weight-loss diets don't. If you cut down too much on what you eat, you'll end up hungry and may eat more than you would have eaten otherwise. Or your body will think that it's starving and will try to protect itself. Your metabolism will slow down, which means your body won't use the calories in food as quickly and may store them as fat. Dieting is especially dangerous during puberty, when your body needs extra energy from food to help you grow.

Focus on changing your habits, not just now but for years to come. Your goal isn't to reach a certain weight as fast as you can. Instead, it's to teach yourself to eat well and get the right amount of exercise—and your weight will naturally go down. This should take several months, but you'll start feeling better almost immediately, and the weight loss will be real and lasting.

Dear American Girl,

I am just 9 years old and weigh too much for my age. My cousins call me names. Once my class got some shirts for the walkathon, and I had to get XL. When we got the shirts, this girl put on my shirt and it looked like a dress on her. My friends started laughing. I was so embarrassed I just wanted to go home and hide under my desk.

Ashamed

Try not to feel like hiding. It's the bullies who should feel ashamed. You might want to talk with your school counselor or another trusted adult about ways to deal with these painful situations. At the same time, talk with your parents and doctor about a healthy, long-term plan for getting your weight down to where it should be for your height and age. The bullies will retreat, and even more important: You will feel like the happy and strong girl you are.

Dear American Girl,

I'm scared, annoyed, and downright embarrassed about my body. I am in sixth grade and am way ahead of almost every girl in school. How do I get guys to stop looking at my breasts and girls to stop calling me names?

Overdeveloped

It may help to know that time is on your side and very soon you won't be so alone. Right now, though, you're in the spotlight. Boys your age are curious about girls' changing bodies, and they're not always good at hiding it. If you notice a boy staring at your chest, say "I really don't like it when you stare at me like that. It feels disrespectful and uncomfortable, and I want you to stop." As for girls, remind them that you're all growing up and that name calling is hurtful. You might get some good suggestions from your mom or an older female friend.

 If the teasing doesn't stop or if you ever feel scared, it's time to talk to a parent, teacher, or school counselor.

The behaviors in the list below are examples of what's called *sexual harassment,* and they're against the law at school. If you're being harassed, the school needs to take action to protect you.

- Making sexual comments or comments about your body
- Whistling or making rude gestures
- Rubbing up against you
- Touching, grabbing, or poking your breasts or other parts of your body

Body Image

Dear American Girl,

I know I am not supposed to compare myself to girls on TV and in magazines. But what if they are much skinnier and prettier than I am?

Maddie

My friends say their clothes look too big for them, and when they say that, I get nervous and embarrassed. It makes me suck in my stomach to make it look like I'm skinny, even though I am not overweight.

Embarrassed

My mom says my body is healthy, but I'm really worried about my weight. I want to be thinner. No matter if I exercise and watch what I eat, still nothing works.

Worried

I am developing slowly. My friends are already growing bigger breasts. When I look in the mirror I think I'm fat, even though I'm not. I know I'm just making myself feel insecure. Why do I do that?

Feeling Insecure

A lot of people say I'm skinny and cute, but inside I feel fat and ugly. How can I make myself confident about my looks?

Confused

Girls can get so used to seeing super-skinny models and actors with perfect skin and hair that they don't realize what's normal and healthy. Also, at your age, a girl's own body is changing so fast it's hard for her to get an accurate sense of what she really looks like. Add in the emotional ups and downs of puberty, and it's easy to see why she can feel insecure about herself. Starting today, stop comparing yourself to media images. They are just that: images. They are not real. Look around, and you'll see that real beauty doesn't fit one mold. Real beauty starts with being healthy and with being true to the body you've got. Treat your body right by eating well and exercising. And treat your spirit right, too. Ask a parent or doctor for an objective opinion if you need it, and surround yourself with girls of all shapes and sizes who are happy with themselves and not trying to look like someone else. You'll find yourself feeling happier and more confident, too.

Moods & Feelings

Letters about mood swings, crushes, and other emotions

Dear American Girl,

I cry a lot for NO reason. My mom says I'm going through hormone changes. I'm very scared. Is this normal?

Confused

I think I have a feeling disorder because I overreact to everything.

Always Exploding

I'm 10, and growing up is pretty hard. I have always been a bit emotional, but this is nuts.

M.R.

My mood has gone wild. Whether I'm feeling angry, sad, frustrated, or lonely, I cry. I know I get enough sleep. What else can I do?

Crying a River

I'm going through a rough time. I go crazy one minute and am calm the next, and then I'm yelling at a boy on the bus. What is wrong with me??

Scared and Worried

Hormones are partly to blame for intense emotions, mood swings, and reactions during puberty. Also, because of the way your brain develops, it is somewhat ruled by emotion through the teen years. As a result, puberty can seem like an emotional roller coaster! Here are a few things you can do to get a grip on your emotions and make the ride smoother.

- Take good care of yourself. If you eat right, get enough sleep, and get enough exercise, your brain will be much more able to cope with stress.

- Take a time-out when you feel your moods swinging or you're overwhelmed, upset, or confused. Some quiet time alone will allow you to gather your thoughts and get calmer before going back out to deal with the world.

- Practice relaxing your body and deep breathing when you wake up and when you go to bed. It will help you fall asleep—and start the morning right. And when stuff happens during the day, you'll be able to calm yourself quickly with a deep breath or two before you react.

- Pay attention to what kinds of things upset you the most. Just being aware can help you cope better because you won't be taken by surprise.

- Do something you love every day. It will help keep your batteries charged with positive energy.

Dear American Girl,

I have to share a room with my sister, and it drives me crazy because I never have a place to escape to.

Leave Me Alone!

As you get older, you want and need times of privacy. You and your sister might agree to certain periods when you could each have the room to yourselves, although those scheduled times might not match up with when you actually need some alone time. Is your room large enough that you could put up a decorative screen or hang a curtain to create visual privacy? Is there another space in your home—such as a spare bedroom, a large closet, or an area in the basement—that you could use, even if you can't officially move in? If the weather is nice, are there outdoor spaces where you like to go on your own? Talk with your parents about your need for privacy, and see if they can help you find solutions—and set up your new space for solitude.

Dear American Girl,

When I was 11, I knew who I was, what my personality was, what makes me ME! When I turned 13 it all changed. I don't know who I am anymore! I lost my personality and can't find myself. I need help!

Who Am I?

During puberty, there's so much change happening so fast it's just hard to keep up with yourself! Also, girls are often under pressure to be somebody that they're not—especially from the media and from other kids. You might even be pressuring yourself to be more grown-up than you're ready to be yet. To find yourself again, try making a list of the things you like, such as, "I like walking my dog. I like to swim. I like to read. I like to wear bright colors. I like to hang out with my cousins." You can do this once, or even keep a journal that you add to whenever you want. Seeing things written down will help you define yourself. You'll also recognize that many of the things that were part of your personality when you were younger are still there. You're still you.

The hormones that are changing your body are also helping you notice and get excited about this cute, sweet, funny guy. We are biologically programmed to have feelings of attraction, which can be the first step to romantic love. While attraction is exciting and fun, it's not the same thing as love, though, and that's important for all girls to keep in mind. Between now and high school, you may be attracted to lots of people. These experiences will help you learn how to respond to your feelings in ways that make you happy and keep you healthy. As you get to know a person, make a habit of asking yourself if you feel respected and understood. If the answer is no, that person isn't right for you. But if it's yes, your attraction may deepen into a genuine relationship.

Dear American Girl,

When I get mad at my dad he just gives me a lecture. I'm positive he knows I'm going through puberty, and I am puzzled as to why he would act like this.

AG Reader

As hard as it is to go through puberty, you're still responsible for the choices you make and the way you behave. Sometimes girls (and boys, too) feel like they have permission to do things they know are wrong, blaming hormones or puberty or "being a teenager." But that's not true. Your job as a teenager is to figure out how to deal with puberty in ways that are more and more mature. And it's your parent's job to help you do that by making rules, setting limits, and enforcing consequences. Instead of getting mad at your dad, try talking with him. You're not expected to be perfect. Just be honest and open, and own your actions. Also, try to remember that kids whose parents have rules and expectations actually have the easiest time getting through puberty.

Dear American Girl,

Some sad things have happened in my family. I cry a lot in my pillow, and I feel better after, but I don't want my friends to see.

Too Many Tears

Talking with someone you trust can help you feel better. This might be a family member or an adult such as a counselor, but it can also be a good friend. If you don't want to be seen crying at school, that's fair. Try not to worry about crying when you're with someone who cares about you, though, in a place where you feel comfortable expressing yourself. Drawing and writing in a journal can also help when you feel sad. At the same time, think of ways you can cheer yourself up. Make plans with friends, create something beautiful, do a sport—anything you enjoy. Although this won't change the sad things that have happened, you'll be able to move forward and feel happier and stronger.

Dear American Girl,

I really need help and advice. I know there are websites that could let me talk to other girls my age, but I'm not sure what they are. Could you help me?

Looking for Answers

When you need help and advice, the first place to turn is to a real person you trust. Depending on your question, that person might be a parent, an older sibling, a teacher, a good friend, your doctor, or someone else you'd consider an expert. Websites can give you extra information, but only if you know the website is reliable. There's no rule or filter to make sure anything on the Internet is trustworthy. Many sites are inaccurate or misleading. Many are trying to sell you something. And with some sites, your privacy or safety is at risk, especially if you're chatting or messaging. Even when a website is reliable, it may not answer your particular question or help you think something through. So line up real-life advisors for advice. And after you've done that, have them help you find good websites for further reading.

Tips for Talking with Parents

Pointers for talking with the adults you trust

It's normal to feel uncomfortable talking with your parents about changes that are happening to your body. But remember that every woman—including your mom and grandma—went through what you're going through now. And dads went through big changes when they were your age, too. Your dad may know more than you think he does, and what he doesn't know, he can help you find out. Your parents can almost always help you solve problems or answer questions, and you'll almost always feel better after talking with them.

If you have a hard time talking with your parents about puberty, try these tips:

1. **Plan ahead.**
   Don't bring up something when your parent is rushing to get out the door. Instead of asking to talk right now, set up a time to talk later. Ask your dad if you can go for a walk after dinner, or let your mom know that you'd like to help with dishes tonight so that the two of you can chat. If the time you suggest won't work, ask when would be a better time.

2. **Pick the right place.**
   Go someplace private, where other family members won't interrupt you. Turn off the TV and your cell phone. If talking face-to-face freaks you out, try talking while riding in the car or sitting side-by-side on your bed.

3. **Keep it simple.**
   Start with how you feel and why, such as, "I feel scared because I may get my period any day" or "I feel embarrassed because my friends wear bras and I don't." Plan your words ahead of time, and practice them in front of a mirror so that it will be easier to say them out loud.

4. Be specific.

What exactly do you need from your parent? Advice about a problem? A shopping trip for a bra or panty liners? A big hug?

5. Wait for a response.

Take a deep breath, and give your parent a chance to think about what you said. Use that time to congratulate yourself on getting the words out. It's not easy, but you did it.

6. Try a new point of view.

If you don't get the response you were hoping for, try to figure out where your parents are coming from. Are they worried about you? Are they afraid you're growing up too fast? These are good questions to ask your parents in starting an honest and open conversation. You might help them see your side of things, too, by asking something like, "Did you ever feel like this when you were my age?" If you and your parents disagree about whether you're ready for something, such as bras or shaving, ask if you can renegotiate in a month or two.

7. Stay connected.

Keep the conversations going. Come up with a signal that means you need to talk, such as a ribbon tied around your bedroom doorknob or a stuffed animal perched on the kitchen counter. Or make weekly dates with your parent. If writing is easier, pass a notebook back and forth. Just keep talking. The more you do it, the easier it gets.

Break the Ice

Having trouble opening your mouth and letting the words flow? Start by asking your mom a few of these questions. Hearing about her experiences when she was your age might make it easier to talk about your own.

"What did you notice first when you started puberty? How did you feel about it?"

"Did you develop earlier, later, or about the same time as your friends?"

"When did you start wearing a bra? Who helped you buy it?"

"How old were you when you got your first period? How did you tell your mom?"

"When did you first start liking someone? Were you embarrassed? What did you do about it?"

"What did you like about the way you looked as a girl? What didn't you like?"

"Did you feel upset or confused a lot when you were my age? Who did you talk to? What helped?"

Isn't it a relief to know that other girls wonder and worry about the same things you do? You're not alone, and you're perfectly normal. Whatever questions you have, you can find the answers. Be confident in your own voice, and keep talking with the people you trust. That's the best way to care for your growing body—and your spirit, too.

Want to write a letter of your own? Send it to:

Is This Normal? Editor
American Girl
8400 Fairway Place
Middleton, WI 53562

All comments and suggestions received by American Girl
may be used without compensation or acknowledgment.
We're sorry, but photos can't be returned.

Here are some other American Girl books you might like:

Each sold separately. Find more books online at americangirl.com.

Parents, request a FREE catalog at **americangirl.com/catalog**.
Sign up at **americangirl.com/email** to receive the latest news and exclusive of

Discover online games, quizzes, activities,
and more at **americangirl.com/play**